If You Can't Say Something Nice, What Do You Say?

Practical Solutions for Working Together Better

Sarita Maybin

2006

If You Can't Say Something Nice, What Do You Say?

If You Can't Say Something Nice, What Do You Say?

TABLE OF CONTENTS

APPENDICES

ABOUT THE AUTHOR...

Sarita Maybin is an award-winning professional speaker whose audiences have fun learning how to stay positive, handle communication challenges and work together better.

Sarita has presented workshops and keynote speeches in 47 states, in nine Canadian provinces, in England, Hong Kong, Singapore, Malaysia, Mexico and Iceland. Some of her clients include NASA, Nokia, Hewlett Packard, Kaiser Permanente, Los Angeles County, PGA, WD-40 and the Las Vegas Convention Center.

Prior to becoming a full-time professional speaker in 1993, Sarita worked in University Administration for thirteen years. She has a B.A. degree in Psychology and an M.A. degree in Counseling both from the University of Maryland, College Park.

For additional information about Sarita Maybin's books, speeches and seminars:
Email SaritaTalk@aol.com, call (800) 439-8248 or visit her website www.SaritaMaybin.com.

PRAISE FOR

If You Can't Say Something Nice, What Do You Say?

"Outstanding! Sarita provides realistic strategies that can be applied immediately to increase your effectiveness in working with people."
-Keith Harrell,
Motivational Teacher and Author, **The Attitude of Leadership**

"Sarita's advice helps you navigate the waters of office relationships. She offers useful strategies for those difficult conversations and provides a fun look at responding to personal criticism."
-Ann Mah,
Past National President, American Business Women's Association

"Sarita Maybin's skillful combination of positive examples and practical phrases will transform your communication experience."
-Les Brown,
Motivational Speaker & Best Selling Author, **It's Not Over Until You Win!**

"Silence may be golden, according to the old adage, but it's also a guarantee that your true thoughts and feelings won't be known. While no one likes confrontation — especially when it's with a boss or a loved one — sometimes these conversations are necessary to resolve important situations and for your own peace of mind. *If You Can't Say Something Nice, What Do You Say?* offers practical, easy-to-implement suggestions on how to deal with these difficult everyday situations without damaging significant workplace and personal relationships."
-Mara Dresner,
Editor, **Strategies**

"If you ever have been faced with what to say to a client, family member, or friend in an uncomfortable situation, this book is for you. Sarita's suggestions will enable you to face these situations with grace and ease. You'll want to keep this book in your briefcase for easy access!"
-Greg Franklin,
Sales Consultant, Keynote Speaker and Contributing Author, **Chicken Soup for the African American Soul**

"I feel my confidence rise with each use of one of Sarita's Top Ten Phrases. The 'confrontation' ends and resolution begins at that moment. It's magical!"
-Kurt Hagel,
Group Director, Downey Savings and Loan

"Finally, a book that provides how-to's that will help you say what needs to be said in a way the listener can hear it! Sarita's easy-to-

remember techniques are a must read for corporate professionals, educators, and counselors."
-Lenora Billings-Harris,
Diversity Consultant and Author, **The Diversity Advantage: A Guide to Making Diversity Work**; 2006-2007 President, National Speakers Association

"Stop wondering what to say and start improving your communication today. Read this book!"
-Jim Cathcart, Author, **Relationship Selling: How To Get and Keep Customers**
President, National Speakers Association, 1988-89

ACKNOWLEDGEMENTS

First, THANK YOU to the clients who have hired me and the participants around the world who have eagerly engaged in my keynotes and seminars. During the 12 years that I have been speaking professionally, it is their stories and willingness to share that has enriched my life in general and my presentations in particular.

I am appreciative of the colleagues with whom I have "master minded" over the years. Seeing them move forward with their books and other worthy projects has inspired me to stay on track with my own endeavors. Thank you Nanci McGraw, Carolyn Gross, Rebecca Everett, Liz Goodgold, Lesa Heebner and Dee Sanford. And, I am grateful for the support of my other colleagues – you know who you are – in the National Speakers Association and in the African American Business Women of Vision group.

Kudos goes to the prolific writer Victoria Moran who helped me figure out how to write a book proposal in 2003 when I was trying to get this book in the hands of a New York publisher. And, of course, I must commend Kristin Nelson of the Nelson Literary Agency for her diligence in pursuing potential publishers for this book.

I acknowledge Mary Marcdante for being the first person to help me realize that I might actually be able to write this book. Her enthusiastic and encouraging reaction to the book's concept and title, "If You Can't Say Something Nice....", way back in 1998 signaled to me that it could be done. I appreciate her insights regarding book proposals as well.

Karen O'Connor's professional editing expertise was a huge help. It was not only the technical aspects of editing that I appreciated but also the encouraging comments about the book's content that kept me going during the writing process. I was especially encouraged by her viewpoint that I should write until I've said what I had to say and not worry about the length of the book.

Andre Augustin has been a true blessing to me. Without his informal feedback, way with words, and nudging along the way this book may never have come to be. His friendship and support have been invaluable as well.

Susan Guzzetta, who has persistently and positively marketed my speaking business, is to be commended. I have appreciated her sales skills, her friendship and her gentle reminders that she could better promote me if I would write THE BOOK!

Teresa Jones and her family have been part of "my village." Without their kindness and caring for my daughter when I traveled on business, I would never have been able to pursue my speaking career. I am deeply indebted to them.

I want to express my gratitude to my family who has both challenged and supported me at just the right times. My sisters, Marlisa and Kristina, my brother Hugo Jr. and my dad Hugo Maybin have all been in my corner when I've needed them most.

And, I want to honor my late mother, Doris Maybin, to whom I am dedicating this book. Last but not least, I am most grateful for and proud of my daughter Melina Anderson, who is now a teenager and makes sure on a daily basis that I practice what I preach!

This book is dedicated to my mother,
the late Doris Maybin (Aug 1929 – July 2005),
from whom I learned to love
the spoken and written word.

CHAPTER 1

To Confront or Not Confront?

What to say and how to say it when you'd rather not say anything at all!

"Believe in yourself. You gain strength, courage and confidence by every experience in which you stop to look fear in the face...you must do that which you think you cannot."
—Eleanor Roosevelt

If you can't say something nice, then don't say anything at all! From the time you were a toddler, you may have been sufficiently brainwashed to believe that line. However, in the adult world you may feel a need to share an opposing thought or two...without destroying the relationship.

At work, there may be people who are not doing their fair share, employees coming in late and bosses stealing the credit for your work.

Outside of work, there may be unsupportive family members, well intentioned friends who question your choices and community members passing judgment.

To confront or not to confront? Most of the time, you would probably rather not have to deal with tough communication situations. And certainly, you'd rather not have to confront them. Or, perhaps you're just not sure how to do it "nicely." So, you contemplate, deliberate and eventually, procrastinate.

F.E.A.R. - Find out what's keeping you from confronting

Avoidance! That seems to be the preferred strategy for dealing with challenging communication situations. Understandably, you would rather not deal with it.

After all, confronting an individual about bothersome behavior or sharing concerns comes with some risks. What if you hurt the other person's feelings? Or even worse, what if the person is offended or becomes defensive? It could get ugly! No wonder most people avoid these situations.

However, if fear is stopping you from handling situations that need to be handled, you must first figure out what exactly it is that scares you. Then, do a "reality check" and see if indeed that fear is valid. Or is it "false evidence?" "False Evidence Appearing Real" is what experts say the acronym F.E.A.R. means. However, I think that for many people the acronym really stands for: "Forget Everything And Run!"

Which of the following keep you from handling challenging situations? And, how likely is that feared outcome?

(Check all that apply.)

__ Hurting person's feelings

__ Retaliation
__ Getting an angry or defensive reaction
__ Getting angry or upset yourself
__ Saying something you will regret
__ Making matters worse
__ Destroying the relationship
__ Saying something that will make you look stupid
__ Jeopardizing your job
__ Being seen as negative

Once again, ask yourself: How likely is the feared outcome? Often, you will never really know the outcome until you actually address the situation. Sometimes you may be completely off base on how the other person will react.

One of my colleagues, Rob, a sales rep, had been seething for weeks after having received a commission check that was $500 less than what he expected. Although he felt extremely angry and cheated, he cringed at the thought of approaching his boss about the discrepancy. Rob convinced himself that there must be some sort of logical explanation.

If Rob had used the fear checklist, he probably would have checked "fear of destroying the relationship" and "fear of being seen as negative." Even though weeks passed and he continued to stew in his anger, he still did not confront the situation. His fear checklist at that point might have included "fear of saying something you will regret" and "fear of getting angry or upset yourself."

By the time I ran into Rob at a business luncheon, he was

so furious about the situation he could spit! I suggested that he give his boss the benefit of the doubt and check out the reason for the commission discrepancy. Perhaps, say something like "I noticed that the amount on my check was $500 less than what I was expecting and I'm wondering if you'd be willing to double check the paperwork?" He called two days later to share that he had used that approach, the boss had checked it out and discovered that there had indeed been a computer error. A $500 check payable to Rob was being processed as we spoke.

Rob took the risk and it paid off – literally! Most of the time, when you confront situations there is some risk involved. As **Difficult Conversations,** the 1999 book based on the work of the Harvard Negotiation Project, states in its introduction "No matter how good you get, difficult conversations will always challenge you. Achieving perfect results with no risk will not happen. Getting better results in the face of tolerable odds might."

In other words, there is no perfect, risk-free strategy. And there is no guarantee that the other person will respond favorably to what you share. This is especially true if you already know, for example, that your boss resists feedback. Or, that your co-worker regularly throws a tantrum when others disagree. And, when you share concerns about a colleague's idea, you run the risk of hurting his or her feelings. But, with the use of certain strategies and skills - many of which are discussed in this book - you may be able to at least increase the chances of achieving the results you want.

BLM (Be Like Me) – When you should NOT confront

When should you not confront a situation? That is really the first question. Just because the other person's way is not your way is a good reason not to confront. Some people suffer from what I call the BLM Syndrome, better known as "Be Like Me" Syndrome. These people spend endless hours confronting and coercing others to change their ways, simply because it is not the way they would do it. If you hear yourself uttering any of the following phrases, you may be suffering from "Be Like me" Syndrome:

"That's dumb!"
"Why do they have to do everything the hard way"
"If only she would..."
"If they would just do what I suggested, it would be much easier"
"He's so hard headed"
"I wouldn't do it that way"

You may have heard the expression "I have a choice. I can be happy or I can be right." How true! Sometimes we make ourselves miserable all in the interest of being right or convincing someone else that our way is the right way. While everything might be "easier" if that other person were not so "hard headed" and would heed your advice, that is not the ideal reason for confronting a situation.

Truth or Consequences –What will it take for you to address the problem?

The most important reason to confront a situation is when the other person's actions are in some way negatively affecting others. There must be some negative impact or consequence that propels you to step forward and tell the truth about the situation. At some point it becomes clear that if you don't tell the truth, you will have to continue to suffer the consequences of not taking action. Rob, the sales rep in the earlier example, knew that if he didn't share how he really felt with his boss, he would continue to be angry and grow resentful. This could eventually affect his attitude and his work.

Most people secretly hope that the annoying situation will either get better or go away. Unfortunately, like dirty dishes piling up in the sink, it only gets worse. As one of my seminar participants put it, "There are only two situations that might get better: 1) The teenager will grow out of it and 2) The boss will eventually retire." However, even in those two cases, it might be an excruciatingly long time between now and then.

So, ask yourself: What are the consequences of NOT confronting the situation? Will the problem fester and grow worse? Will it begin to affect your attitude and taint the way you interact with that person? If so, it may be time to tell the truth.

Use A.I.R. – A Three Step Process for Sharing Concerns

When you are ready to confront, use AIR: A- Awareness, I- Impact, R- Request. This three-step model for constructively

confronting a negative situation can be a great tool in a variety
of challenging situations.

AWARENESS –

Assume that other people are not aware that what they are
doing is a problem. Give them the benefit of the doubt. Sometimes participants in my workplace negativity workshops tell me
that they were sent to the seminar to get their negative attitudes
"fixed." Many of them also quietly confess that they were not
aware of the negative impact of their behavior. They had been
walking around with the proverbial spinach in their teeth and
no one had told them.

Following are possible phrases that you can use to make the
other person aware of your concerns and also give him or her
the benefit of the doubt. As with all phrases presented in this
book, you are encouraged to choose the ones you like the best,
and ignore the rest.

"Awareness" phrases include:

"I don't know if you're aware of it…"
"I'm sure that it wasn't your intention to…"
"Perhaps you didn't realize that…"
"As you may already know…"
"I noticed that…"
"I'm getting the impression that…"
"It seems like…"

IMPACT–

(Also known as the consequence that causes you to want to tell the person the truth).

This second step is a great litmus test if you are still unsure whether or not to confront. This is the "so what?" question. Why confront? Oh yeah, that's right – the person's behavior is negatively affecting you or others. It's NOT just that you're thinking, "I wish this person would be like me" (BLM). This is the time to share with the other person HOW the behavior is negatively impacting you, the team, or whomever it affects. Sometimes his or her behavior may even be having a negative impact on that person (for example – "When you turn in your part of the project late and we miss the deadline, I'm concerned that it makes us both look unprofessional.")

"Impact" phrases include:

"I'm concerned that…"
"I worry that…"
"I feel that…"
"When you do _____ it makes me feel _____"
"When you say _____ the way it affects the office…"
"I feel _____ if you do _____"

REQUEST –
(NOT a demand)
Specifically, what do you want the person to do differently next time? In what way would you like him or her to change?

This step is the most overlooked of the three steps. It is easy for most people to identify what they don't want. For example: "I wish my co-workers would stop complaining all the time." But what do you want them to do instead? Keep concerns to themselves? Find a positive way to express their concerns? Complain to the boss or someone who can change things? Figure out solutions to the concerns? The list of possible changes is long. Most people are not mind readers, so you must let them know what YOUR preference is.

By the way, standing in the middle of the office and muttering to no one in particular, "Sure would be nice if someone would answer the phone," does not count as a request.

This notion of making a request can be especially problematic — and perhaps, even amusing — if we look at the "Mars-Venus" angle. You may recognize the scenario of the husband and wife driving past the fast food restaurant. The wife says, "Honey, are you hungry?" He says "No" and keeps driving. He wonders why she gives him the cold shoulder for the rest of the ride home. Surely, he must have intuited that her question "Honey, are you hungry?" was not a rhetorical one. Actually, it was not even a literal question. It was a disguised request for action. Translation: "I am hungry. Let's stop so that I can get something to eat." Requests must be clear and direct!

"Request" phrases include:

"Would you be willing to…"
"Could you please…"
"In the future I would like you to…"

"Next time I would appreciate..."

"I really need your help with..."

"I would rather you..."

Or, if you want to request input regarding future action, use:

"Would you be willing to agree to..."

"How can we resolve this?"

"What are our options?"

"Would you consider..."

"Would it be possible to..."

"Let's..."

"Can we..."

Let's Make a Deal – Try new strategies. Get New Results.

"Can I trade my job for what's behind door # 2?" a woman in one of my workshops joked. (OK, maybe she was serious). One of the comments that I hear most frequently from people who are in jobs that they dislike or jobs where there are hard-to-please people is: "If I could find another job, I'd leave."

Sure, there are bosses from hell and co-workers who are jerks. This is probably a valid reason for wanting to look elsewhere for work instead of staying and dealing with the existing situation. However, you can run but you can't hide! You might be able to find a better job tomorrow, but within weeks of arriving at your new job you'll probably find that the new job has difficult people too. The names have changed, but the behaviors that annoy you remain the same.

Several years ago I attended a series of self-development workshops through Landmark Education. I was particularly jolted by a comment that the instructor made about people who keep changing jobs, changing their living situations and changing their relationships in the hopes of finding something "better." He pointed out that it sometimes seems as though history keeps repeating itself, over and over. The same kinds of clashes, conflicts and crises keep occurring. Why? As he put it: "No matter where you go, there YOU are!"

This reminds me of the words of Dr. Susan Jeffers, author of the book **Feel the Fear and Do It Anyway:**

"If you always do what you've always done, you'll always get what you've always gotten."

It is my hope that you'll try some new strategies — perhaps a few from this book — and get new results!

RECAP – Chapter 1: To Confront or Not to Confront?

1. **F.E.A.R** – False Evidence Appearing Real? Or Forget Everything and Run? Use the FEAR checklist to see what's keeping you from confronting tough situations.

2. Avoid **"Be Like Me" (BLM)** – Don't confront just because they're not doing it your way. (i.e. - "If only they would do it my way...," "That's dumb!")

3. Use **A.I.R.:** A three-step process for sharing concerns

   Awareness – "You may not realize...," "I'm sure it wasn't your intention to..."

   Impact – "When you do that, the way it impacts me is...," "I'm concerned..."

   Request – "Next time, could you...," "Would you be willing to?" "Let's..."

4. Ask yourself: What is the consequence of NOT confronting?

5. Try New Strategies. Get New Results.

CHAPTER 2

Is the Glass Half Empty or Half Full?

How to set the stage for positive communication

"Real life isn't going to be perfect, but the recurring knowledge of what is working in our lives can help us not only survive, but surmount our difficulties." - Sarah Ban Breathnach, Author, **Simple Abundance**

Four Year Olds

When my daughter was born fourteen years ago, it occurred to me that I knew nothing about child rearing. Sure, I had been a working person and supervisor for many years, but my expertise on children was limited. Being the good educator that I was, I decided to do some research -- a one year subscription to various parenting magazines. One of the juicy nuggets of wisdom frequently shared in these magazines:

"By the age of four, your child's personality is formed. That's who he or she is going to be FOREVER!"

Yikes! Many intimidating thoughts such as this one jumped from the pages, but I continued to read month after month. A startling realization occurred to me at the end of my one-year subscription: In reading these parenting magazines, I had learned more about how to handle my co-workers than I had about raising my daughter!!!

Here's an experiment: Next time you walk into the office, you will run into that challenging person — you know, the one whose voice sounds to you like that of the teacher in the Peanuts cartoons: "Wah wah wah!" When you hear that voice, don't react or let this person predictably push your buttons. Instead, just look at the person. And, in your mind I'd like you to be thinking:

HE'S BEEN THIS WAY SINCE HE WAS FOUR YEARS OLD!

Fourteen years ago, this was my big wake up call! Who do I think I am that I can go to one seminar or read one book and then try to change this person? How empowering for me to realize that this person has been this way for a very long time! What a relief to decide that it was no longer in my job description to try to change or fix this person! When changing and fixing the other person is no longer the goal, this certainly sets the stage for positive communication.

Filling the Half Empty Glass

Another way to set the stage for positive communication is to change "half empty" thinking to "half full" thinking. How many times have you said something such as:

"He's so arrogant!" or "She's so indecisive."

Here's a thought: How about changing the negative interpretation of "arrogant" to a neutral or positive such as "He knows his abilities" or "He's self-confident." OR....changing

"She's indecisive" to "She's open to new ideas" or "She's flexible."

Here are a few more:
"Penny Pincher" becomes "uses resources wisely" or "efficient"
"Goes along with the crowd" becomes "willingly participates" or "cooperative"
"Pest" becomes "persistent", "interested", "involved", "eager"

Convert the following items from "half empty" to "half full":
"Nitpicker"
"Impulsive"
"Hyperactive"

As you can guess, it's hard to have positive communication when the backdrop in your mind is a negative one. Imagine the voice in the back of your mind shouting PEST even as you are saying to a colleague "I'd love to collaborate with you." In fact, one of the biggest challenges in communication is when you want to say something "nice" but your thoughts are quite the contrary.

The Evil Twin
I am convinced there is the voice of a long lost evil twin in the back of my mind. This is the critical and judgmental voice that whispers things that are not so nice. You know the voice. The one that would have you say things that would surely mean the demise of your business and personal relationships.

Do you recognize below any of these questionable phrases that may loiter in the back of your mind?

"Whatever!"
"Like that will ever happen!"
"It's not my problem"
"Fine! I'll show them"
"That will never work"
"Why bother, things will never change anyway"
"It figures"
"What an arrogant _____!"
"She's such a pest!"

I often wondered where such phrases originate. I found my answer. In the hundreds of seminars I've conducted over the past 12 years, I've noticed a recurring theme. It seems to be directly related to the negative voice emanating from the back of the mind. The theme: Resentment. When I asked seminar participants how they and their workplace colleagues might complete a hypothetical survey question: "I resent the fact that..." here's what I heard:

I resent the fact that...
- My ideas are not heard
- My boss doesn't acknowledge or appreciate me
- My boss steals credit for my ideas
- Coworkers are slacking off and no one is doing anything about it
- My company is changing and I have no information
- My company is reorganizing my dept but no one asked for my input
- Clients are making demands, but company policy or

lack of resources makes it impossible for me to satisfy the client
- My boss doesn't back up my decisions

By the way…change the words "boss", "company", "clients" to "husband", "wife", "mother-in-law" and "friends" and we still come up the theme: resentment. It's no wonder that voice is alive and well with negative things to say.

The Three P's for Staying Positive

"How do I keep the contagious effect of all this negativity from rubbing off on me?" is the question that I get asked most frequently by my seminar participants. My reply: The Three P's. These were inspired by the work of Dr. Martin Seligman who has extensively studied what makes some people positive despite the most dire circumstances. And, likewise, what makes some people consistently negative no matter what positive things may come their way. The key is to ask yourself these three questions:

Is it **personal**?

When the company downsizes, when the boss throws a tantrum or when the co-worker in the next cubicle grumbles in response to your morning greeting, ask yourself: "Are any of these really about me?" Most of the time you will discover that in fact you cannot – and should not – own that negativity. A comment in a popular women's magazine was quite telling. It said "You would be depressed if you knew how seldom people were really thinking about you." In other words, it is NOT about you as much as you may think it is.

Is it **permanent**?

The popular expression "This too shall pass" applies here. The extent to which you can see the "light at the end of the proverbial tunnel" is the extent to which you can remain positive…in spite of all. On the other hand, those who dwell on the negative side are likely to think "I see the light at the end of the tunnel. It looks like an oncoming train to me."

Does it matter in the big **picture**?

A man in one of my seminars told me that, unlike his colleagues who had been sent to my seminar to get their negative attitudes "fixed," he was attending to learn how to "fix" his boss. When I inquired about the boss' shortcomings he said, "My boss chews me out in the hallway daily, just for sport!" I asked how he managed to stay positive in spite of this daily Dilbert style dressing down. "When my boss is screaming, turning bright red, veins bulging in his forehead, I simply look at him," he said, "and in the back of my mind I'm thinking When they record the history of time, will THIS event be documented? NOT!"

Counteract the Negatives – Options, Options, Options

In the mid 1980's I was working as a department director at a medium sized state university. At that time, most of the staff felt that universities were immune to the downsizing trend that had begun gaining momentum. So you can imagine our shock when a newly hired university president began slashing jobs campus wide. A fear and panic set in. A dark cloud hung over the campus. I recall that everyone I encountered seemed to have an undercurrent of gloom and doom.

It occurred to me this was a situation where I could not change the negativity. My only recourse was to COUNTER-ACT it. You can do the same. Find other ways to counteract the non-negotiable negatives. Better yet, find a positive option that might also provide a financial fall back plan in case you lose your job!

Thus, my new "moonlight" as a part time Mary Kay Cosmetics consultant was created. I remember my academic colleagues teasing "You're peddling lipsticks?! Everything is so pink! And, so perky!" My reply: "I need pink and perky to counteract the negativity! Plus, it is my back up plan. What's yours?"

Even though some of my colleagues would not have chosen the same alternate job that I did, they did understand that it was really about having options. That's what keeps you from feeling like your back is against the wall and you have no where to go. Have you ever noticed the most negative people are those who feel that they have no choices? They feel stuck. When you think about a current unsatisfactory situation that you're in, what are YOUR options?

W.I.I.F.M.

My favorite acronym: W.I.I.F.M? What's in it for me? I find it fascinating that all of the behavioral scientists who have studied human behavior over the years have concluded one thing: Human beings do whatever they do based on their answer to the question: What's in it for me? Sometimes this is interpreted as a negative or selfish motivation. But, it's neither negative nor positive. It is just human nature.

Often, I am hired by organizations where there is low morale and high negativity. They ask me to help employees look for strategies to turn negativity into possibility. For many the challenge is to identify what are the positives in the situation. Some of their replies include:
- I like the people I work with

- I feel that what I do in my job is important
- Great benefits
- This job is a stepping stone to where I want to go
- I enjoy the customers
- I'm learning a lot in this job

Think about a negative work or personal situation of your own. What's in it for YOU to stay in that situation?

Get a life!

Several years ago I had an opportunity to conduct training for a large organization known for its conflict and workplace drama. "Take names!" my client told me. "What!" I was puzzled by this request. Apparently, he wanted me to take down the name of anyone in the training who seemed particularly "volatile." I did not fully embrace this idea, but proceeded with the training.

About half way through the day-long workshop, one of the men in that day's group of 30 participants, said "You know, Sarita, when I'm lying awake at night, I think about this place.... When I'm at the grocery store, I think about this place....When I'm walking down the street, I think about this place".... I'm thinking: "Where's my pen and paper? I need to write his name down!"

As my 14 year old daughter would have said "He was creeping me out!"

Just as I was contemplating my next move, the other 29 workshop participants shouted at this man in unison, as though they had choreographed it: "GET A LIFE!" I could not have said it better myself. Speaking as a recovering workaholic, I know first hand that when all you do is work, every little job related problem or disappointment looms larger than life. You end up like this man, thinking about your work in the grocery store because you have nothing else to fill your thoughts.

By the way, I did not write down the man's name. The group was quite generous in helping me engage him in a discussion of possibilities for broadening the scope of his life beyond work. The goal is really not to have all of your "emotional eggs in one basket."

In fact research has shown that people who have balanced lives – family, career, hobbies, friends – fare better because anytime one area is not going so well, you can look to another area to bolster your confidence, self esteem and sense of well-being.

RECAP – Chapter 2: Is the Glass Half Empty or Half Full?

I. Remember...they've been that way since they were four years old. Can you really fix or change them?

2. Convert "half empty" thinking to "half full." For example, she is not a "pest;" she is "persistent." He is not "hyperactive;" he is "enthusiastic!"

3. Beware the "evil twin," that voice in your head that automatically responds with negative thoughts such as "whatever" or "that won't work."

4. Ask yourself the "three P" questions in order to stay positive:

    Is it personal?

    Is it permanent?

    Does it matter in the big picture?

5. If you can't change a negative situation, counteract it! Find positive outlets that balance out the negative situation. Look for other options.

6. Ask yourself WIIFM? (i.e. – "What's in it for me" to stay in this negative situation?)

7. Get a life!

CHAPTER 3

From Conflict to Collaboration

How to turn potentially negative situations into opportunities for partnership

"Those who master others have force; those who master themselves have power." — *Lao Tzu, The Tao of Power*

Workplace Woes

Some of the most common annoyances I've experienced or heard from my seminar participants regarding people at work include:

"She's always complaining and it's starting to drag everyone down."

"He keeps interrupting me when I'm talking at meetings."

"One of my employees has started coming in later and later every day."

"My co-worker misses deadlines which delays my project completion."

"That certain person is spending too much time hanging out in my office and I can't get my work done."

Let's take a look at a couple of potential responses for each of these situations. As you look at the possible replies, you'll notice that the format resembles the A.I.R. model discussed in Chapter I:

Awareness – Does he know that what he's doing is a problem?

Impact - What is the negative effect of his behavior?

Request - What would you like him to do differently in the future?

Dilemma: "She's always complaining and it's starting to drag everyone down."

Possible Replies:

"I've noticed that you frequently mention what's wrong with this department and it's starting to negatively affect some of our attitude's about working here. Can we focus instead on what's right in our dept?"

or....

"It seems like we spend hours every day discussing the downsizing and it's starting to become depressing. I'd rather talk about what our options are."

Dilemma: "He keeps interrupting me when I'm talking at meetings."

Possible replies:

"I don't know if you're aware of it; at meetings you often start talking before I'm finished. I find the meetings to be unproductive when more than one person is trying to talk at the same time. At the next meeting, would you be willing to go for one person speaking at a time?"

or...

"I'm sure you didn't realize it but at the meeting this morning, you interrupted me several times. It made me feel like you didn't want to hear what I had to say. I'd really appreciate your hearing me out next time."

Dilemma: "One of my employees has started coming in later and later every day."

Possible Replies:

"I noticed that you have been coming in later and later over the past few months. As I'm sure you know, our newer employees respect you and look up to you. I'm concerned that if they see you arriving late, they might view it as OK. I really need your help in setting a positive tone in the department by coming in on time."

or...

"Making a good impression with clients is extremely important, as I'm sure you know. When you come in late, clients have to wait and that creates a negative impression. I need you to be here to open the office on time in the future. And, I'm sure the clients would appreciate it too."

Dilemma: "My co-worker misses deadlines which delays my project completion."

Possible Replies:

"I know you realize how important this project is. So, when you turn in your part of the project late and we miss the deadline, it makes us both look bad. Can I count on you next time to get your part to me on time?"

or...

"We both know this project is top priority. Unfortunately, when I get your info late, I can't make my deadline. Tell me what I can do to help out. I really want us to get back on schedule."

Dilemma: "That certain person is spending too much time hanging out in my office and I can't get my work done."

Possible Replies:

"I love chatting with you. Unfortunately, I'm enjoying our chats so much I'm getting behind on my work. Let's schedule a regular time during the lunch hour to get caught up."

or...

"I seem to be doing more socializing than working. I'm going to have to wean myself off of our chats in the future so that I can get out of here by 5pm. Can you help me on that?"

"Green Jello" Principles of Conflict Resolution

One of the most crucial skills in turning conflict into collaboration with those at work —and outside of work too — is the ability to effectively resolve conflict. Here are two key principles of conflict resolution:

Principle #1:   **Figure out the REAL agenda**

Often the real —sometimes hidden — agenda in a conflict is something like ego, turf, power, control or other self-serving issues. You may have noticed this both at work and at home.

Principle #2:   **Have a plan B (or C, D…)**

When you go into a conflict situation, do you just have one idea about how the conflict might be resolved? If so, you may find yourself getting "ugly" and inflexible when the other person chooses not to "buy into" your way of doing things. It's always helpful to have a plan b, c, d….

My big epiphany regarding the two principles came on a Sunday morning ten years ago. I was standing in the kitchen fixing breakfast. This is always a big deal because I don't cook a big breakfast every day. Just on Sundays.

My daughter, who was four years old at the time, came into the kitchen, opened the refrigerator and noticed a four-pack of green jello.

"Mommy," she asked "May I have a green jello?"

At this point I hesitated, contemplating whether or not I wanted her to have it. After all, I was fixing breakfast. However, I said "OK, you may have one."

She took the jello, slurped it up and returned only moments later.

"May I have another one?"

This time I said "No!"

She dropped to the floor in a tantrum. She shrieked in a high pitched, shrill, whiny voice that sounded like fingernails scratching against a chalkboard.

"I want jello, I want jello!"

As my daughter writhed on the floor in a full blown tantrum, I looked at her. Without sympathy, I said "Crying will not help you!"

Let's talk now about the husband.

Husband (shouting from the living room): "Give her the @*# jello!"

Sarita: "Honey, I'd rather not give it to her. I'm fixing breakfast."

Husband: "What's the BIG DEAL! Just give her the jel-lo!"

Sarita: "I'd rather not."

Do you sense a conflict brewing?

At that point, husband and I are at each other's throats.

"Jello!"

"No jello!"

"Jello!"

"No jello!"

"What's wrong with this picture?" I asked myself. "I make a living teaching others conflict resolution, teamwork, dealing with negativity, and communication skills. Surely I was NOT engaged in a conflict over..."GREEN JELLO!!!?"

Then it occurred to me. The two important aspects of conflict resolution. Or, as I now call them: The "green jello" principles!

Principle #1: Figure out the REAL AGENDA

So...what might have been husband's not so hidden agenda in this Sunday morning scenario?

You guessed it...SHUT THE CHILD UP!

And, what might have been my agenda? When I've shared this story in my presentations I have heard many speculations about my REAL agenda:

"I'm cooking breakfast over this hot stove...somebody better eat!" (Ego)
"Crying will NOT be rewarded!" (Discipline)
"I'm the mommy here!" (Control)
"I want those other jellos for myself!" (Self Serving)
"Shut husband up!" (Power/Turf)

This is no different than how conflict happens outside of the kitchen and inside the workplace. Coworkers may say: "Our department can't support that program because of pressing deadlines for our priority projects!" Yet, what they may really mean is:

"You didn't help us with our project last year, so we're not going to help YOU!" (Self serving)

"That project should really be ours!" (Ego, turf)

"If we can't do the project the way we want we don't want to be part of it!" (Control)

Often it's not about the proverbial green jello at all. Yet, many times we get caught up in the superficial and overlook the real underlying issues. The solution in this type of situation is to ask questions and explore further.

Key phrases for digging beneath the surface to find out what's really going on are:

"I'm getting the impression that…"

"I'm sensing that…"

"I noticed _____ and I'm wondering _____."

"It seems like…"

"What else concerns you?"

"I feel like there's more to this than meets the eye."

"I feel like there's something else bothering you."

Principle #2:   Have a plan B (or C, D…)

Isn't it interesting that we often bring only one option to the table in a conflict situation, especially at work. The goal then, is to have as many options in mind as possible AND be open to options that may be proposed by the other person. Have you noticed that the most negative and desperate people are those who feel they have no choices? The more choices and options you have the more positive you can be in general, and the more productive in resolving conflicts.

This brings me back to the kitchen that Sunday morning ten years ago.

Husband's agenda was peace and quiet...and perhaps some need to control the situation.

My agenda ranged from discipline and control to my own self-serving goal of hoarding the jello for myself.

So...the million-dollar question: What plan b, or plan c, will address these multiple agendas?

WHAT ARE THE OPTIONS?

Those who have heard me tell this story have shared many possible options:

"Just let her eat all four jellos."

"Tell her she can have more jello after breakfast."

"Get on the floor and cry with her."

"Send her to a 'time out.'"

"Distract her with something else to do."

"Dump all the jellos out."

"Tell the husband to get her the jello himself."

"Let her eat the jello for breakfast and have the breakfast later."

And, my all time favorite suggestion:

"Go to McDonalds for a Happy Meal and leave husband and daughter home!"

That Sunday morning, I contemplated the many strategies available to me. "If you can get up off the floor and act like a big girl," I said to my daughter, "then you can assist me in preparing breakfast." (That's the "Distract her with something else" option.)

She leapt up from the floor, happy to help me with breakfast. Once again, it wasn't about the green jello. Conflict resolved. Peace and quiet for husband. No spoiled appetite and the remaining three jellos still intact. The next time you find yourself in a conflict – in the kitchen or in the staff meeting – dig beneath the superficial "green jello." Use key phrases such as "it seems like" and "I'm getting the impression..." to figure out the real agenda. Explore the possible angles by asking such questions as:

"What are our options?"
"How can we resolve this?"
"How can we make this work?"
"What do you need from me?"
"Could you live with it if we...."
"How might we gain your cooperation?"

"What do you think about...."

Time Out

Speaking of tantrums and time out, it may be tempting to have a toddler-like reaction when co-workers and others push your buttons. Someone once said "Speak in anger and you'll make the best speech you'll ever regret." I would be remiss if I didn't include this brief section on how to keep your emotions in check when you're trying to move from conflict to collaboration.

"How do I get rid of my urge to burst into tears when someone makes me upset?" was a question asked by one of my seminar participants. My answer to her: "Unfortunately you don't." If she's been responding that way since she was a child (four years old, perhaps?), then it's unlikely that she will completely re-program herself. The key is that she KNOWS how she typically responds and can do something to pre-empt the response...temporarily. Then she can run to the ladies' room and have a good cry. Or in your case, it may be run to your office and pound your desk.

In the meantime, what do you do as you face the designated villain and feel your blood pressure rising? I've provided below a variety of strategies that have been tested and proven by seminar participants. And, I've thrown in a few of my own. Remember, these are just stop-gap measures to help you keep your cool...for now. Eventually, you will need to revisit some of the phrases in this book and use them to initiate a positive discussion. Until then, use the ideas below that work for you.

How to stay calm and keep your cool in a conflict:

- Take deep breaths.

- Count to 10. Or better yet, count backwards.

- Envision a large wart on the person's nose. Or, envision anything that will distract you from your angst.

- Picture the person as a caricature or cartoon.

- Squeeze a muscle, preferably one that is not visible (clenching the jaw doesn't qualify; the offending person can see it). Fingernails into the palms of the hand works.

- Push the imaginary "mute button"; the person's mouth is moving but you don't hear a sound.

- Drink some water – I'm told you can't drink water and cry at the same time. And, you can't say something you might regret either.

- Envision a pleasant scene – your most recent vacation, smiling faces of your kids

- "Velcro moment" – One person told me she coped by picturing herself sticking her coworker by his Velcro covered back onto a Velcro covered wall and leaving him hanging there.

- Revisit the 3 P's for staying positive from Chapter 2. Ask yourself:

Is this personal? Is it permanent? Does it matter in the big picture?

A woman in one of my workshops shared with the group that when she is being yelled at by her boss she says to herself "Could be worse. I could be married to him." Another woman in the room who IS married to someone who yells, chimed in "Even then it could be worse, you could BE him!"

Perhaps, best of all for keeping things in perspective, is remembering the Eleanor Roosevelt quote:

"If you approach each new person in a spirit of adventure, you will find yourself endlessly fascinated by the new channels of thought, experience, and personality that you encounter."

RECAP – Chapter 3: From Conflict to Collaboration

I. **Workplace Woes** - When addressing such issues as:

"She's always complaining and it's starting to drag everyone down."
"He keeps interrupting me when I'm talking at meetings."
"One of my employees has started coming in later and later every day."

Remember to revisit the A.I.R. Model from Chapter I. Ask: Is he aware that he's causing a problem? What is the impact of his behavior? What's your request for change?

2. Two **"Green Jello"** Principles of Conflict Resolution:

Principle # I – Find out the REAL agenda.
Dig beneath the surface by saying:
"I'm getting the impression that..."
"What else concerns you?"

Principle # 2 - Have a Plan B (or C, or D....)
Explore options with the other person by asking:
"How can we resolve this?"
"What are our options?"

3. **Time Out**

When you're in the middle of a conflict situation and can't physically leave, use creative strategies to give yourself a mental "time out." For example, picture the other person as a cartoon, in your head count backwards from ten, and push the imaginary "mute" button.

CHAPTER 4

The Bearer of Bad News

How to give negative feedback in a tactful way that does not destroy the relationship

"You may not think you can reach it. Climb anyway. You may not think you'll be heard. Speak anyway. You may not think you can change things. Try anyway." —Maya Angelou

Top Ten Phrases

Several years ago, one of my clients asked me "Of all the phrases that you share in your seminars, which are your top 10 favorites?" It prompted me to select the phrases listed on the next page. These are especially useful in difficult communication situations. And the phrases allow you to do the following:

- Give the benefit of the doubt

- Seek input

- Take responsibility

- Work together

Sarita's Top 10 Positive Communication Phrases

- **Give benefit of the doubt...**

10. "You may not realize..."
9. "Are you aware of the effect...?"

- **Seek input...**

8. "Help me understand"
7. "I need your help"
6. "I noticed...and I'm wondering"
5. "Would you be willing to...?"

- **Take responsibility...**

4. "I'm concerned..."
3. "I would appreciate..."

- **Work together...**

2. "How can we resolve this...?"
1. "What will it take...?"

Which of the top 10 phrases could you use in your work or personal life? Make a note of what situations you'd use the phrases in and with whom.

Following are examples of how each the top 10 phrases can be used to promote positive communication and tactfully provide negative feedback:

- **Give the benefit of the doubt.**

These two phrases presume that the other person was not aware of the negative impact of his behavior. Remember the "A" Awareness in the A.I.R. model discussed in Chapter I? You may recall from that first chapter the so-called negative people who were sent to my seminar to get fixed. You know, the ones walking around with the proverbial spinach in their teeth and don't even know it. The ones who are talked about in the break room at work, but no one has the nerve or motivation to share concerns with them directly. So, if you wish to clue them in you could say:

10. **"You may not realize…"** and
9. **"Are you aware of the effect?"**

"You may not realize that when you come in late it throws everyone's schedule off."

"You may not realize that the customer's first impression is based on talking with you."

"Are you aware of the effect of your rolling your eyes in the staff meeting?"

"Are you aware of the effect of words like "whatever!" or "like that will work"?

- **Seek input.**

These phrases focus on soliciting the other person's thoughts rather than imposing your views or passing judgment. And, that's especially hard when the other person has done something that annoys you.

8. "Help me understand"

This is a perfect phrase for finding out what a coworker or boss was thinking when he made a certain decision or chose a particular point of view. For example:

"Help me understand the best way to implement this new policy."

"Help me understand what concerns you about my proposal."

"Help me understand what would work best for your dept."

7. "I need your help"

This is a powerful phrase and is especially helpful when you anticipate resistance. You could say:

"I need your help to make this project a success."

"I need your help to complete our assignment on time."

"I need your help if we are to successfully reorganize the department."

6. "I noticed...and I'm wondering"

I call this my "neutral observation" phrase. It allows you to point out what you're seeing and then ask for clarification. When I worked in university administration, I had an employee who used to sit in staff meetings sighing and rolling her eyes whenever she was not happy with the decisions being made. I would say to her "I noticed that you reacted and I'm wondering what your concerns are." She would say "Oh, nothing." She never confessed publicly. But, she did occasionally pull me aside and share her concerns privately. Most importantly, I wanted her – and the rest of the staff – to know that I noticed the reaction and addressed it.

Similarly, you can use this phrase to say such things as:

"I noticed that you weren't at the meeting and I'm wondering what happened."

"I noticed that you sighed when I mentioned our project and I'm wondering what's up."

"I noticed that you mentioned problems and I'm wondering what might be some possible solutions."

5. "Would you be willing to..."

This phrase allows you to make a request rather than demand something. Remember the "R" Request in the "A.I.R." model? This is especially important when you are talking with a client or someone at a higher level in the organization. For example:

"Would you be willing to accept the products next Monday morning instead of Friday?"

"Would you be willing to notify us if there is a delay?"

"Would you be willing to send someone from your department to assist us?"

- **Take responsibility.**

It's easy to point the finger and say "You idiots! You screwed up! It's your fault!" It's more difficult, yet more positive, to take ownership for what bothers you. You could say:

4. "I'm concerned..."

"I'm concerned that I was not consulted in advance."

"I'm concerned that the problem was not resolved."

"I'm concerned that the delay will affect our shipment date."

3. "I would appreciate..."

"I would appreciate your checking with me in advance next time."

"I would appreciate your letting me know if you need help."

"I would appreciate a phone call if there will be a delay."

- **Work together.**

2. "How can we resolve this..."

"How can we resolve this situation so that both our needs are met?"

"How can we resolve this problem most efficiently?"

"Mr. Client, how can we resolve this problem to your satisfaction?"

I. "What will it take..."

"What will it take to regain your trust?"

"What will it take to get your department's support?"

"What will it take to get your business?"

Email me at SaritaTalk@aol.com to let me know which of the top ten phrases are YOUR favorites! Or, perhaps you have additional phrases that you'd like to share. Also, see Appendix I: 105 Phrases for All Occasions at the end of this book.

Feedback Do's & Don'ts – How do you rate?

Here's an opportunity to see how well you're already giving feedback or constructive criticism. CHECK the following items on the "DO" list that you feel you already do well.

DO...

____ Discuss in private

____ Use "I" statements
("I'm concerned", "I would appreciate", "I need you to...")

____ Seek Clarification ("Help me understand...")

____ Confirm understanding ("So what you're saying is...)

____ Explain how behavior affects you or others

____ Seek Solutions/Action ("How can we resolve...", "What would you be willing...")

____ Maintain perspective/sense of humor

Do Maintain a Sense of Humor

Before we take a look at the "Don't" list, I think the last item -- sense of humor -- on the "Do" list above warrants special mention. Personally, I have found keeping a sense of humor to be critical in coping with difficult situations. And, I have asked participants in my workshops to share with me their favorite examples of humor in the workplace.

My first place winner for the best use of humor at work is an airline ticket agent in Denver. He shared with the seminar group the challenge he faces daily with customers in "melt down mode" because they have missed their flights, or worse, had flights cancelled.

The ticket agent then went on to tell us about one specific irate customer — a male celebrity. He wouldn't tell us which male celebrity but he did describe the man's behavior. He told us that the man shouted "You incompetent people! What's the matter with you! Don't they train you?! Why can't your airline get its act together? Can't they coordinate their flights so that we don't miss them...?" On and on the celebrity ranted, finally culminating his tirade by asking the ticket agent, "Do you know who I am?!" The ticket agent said that he paused for just a moment and then replied: "OH NO! Not ANOTHER person today who doesn't know who he is!"

This was a risky response indeed. Yet, the outcome was positive. The ticket agent shared that the man's jaw dropped in response to the comment. Then he fell all over himself apologizing. The unexpected injection of humor had yanked the man out of his downward spiral and allowed the ticket agent to set the tone for a problem solving session. And, by the way, the celebrity's ranting is a perfect demonstration of how you should NOT share feedback or concerns.

That brings us to the "don't" list. Here are the things that you should NOT do when giving negative feedback or constructive criticism:

DON'T...

___ Don't point finger/blame

____ Don't make it personal

____ If possible, don't confront in front of others

____ Don't dictate - AVOID "you" statements like "You better", "You should", "You need to"

____ Don't drop hints or use sarcasm

____ Don't argue

____ Don't name names

____Don't expect immediate change

Don't Use Sarcasm

Let's take a moment to examine one important item on the "don't" list – sarcasm. To explain why sarcasm doesn't work, I must share with you what used to happen when I was a cigarette smoker years ago.

Someone would invariably find my cigarette smoke offensive but would not want to share that feedback with me directly. Instead, the person would drop hints...fake coughing and frantic waving of the hands as if to fan away the smoke. What do you think I REALLY wanted to do in response?

YES! My evil twin desperately wanted to blow the smoke in his or her face. But I did not. I did wish that the person had shared with me directly his or her concerns about the smoke.

The point is that every time you drop hints or use sarcasm in an attempt to give feedback, it evokes the "blow the smoke in your face" or "backatcha" instinct.

Think about the last time someone walked into a meeting late. Someone already seated might have said something in a sarcastic tone like "Oh, nice of you to join us!" Or, better yet, someone you live with walks in the door at midnight after having promised to be home by 9pm. You say sarcastically: "I see you remembered where you live!"

In both of these examples, the recipient of the snide remark will feel the urge to respond by blowing the proverbial smoke in your face. People would prefer that if you have something to say, you say it directly. And say it respectfully, with good intent...and without sarcasm. Revisit the top 10 list to get an idea of what you could use instead of sarcasm. For instance, in the situations above, alternatives might be:

"I was concerned when you didn't arrive at 9pm. I'd certainly appreciate your giving me a quick call when you'll be running late."

"I'm concerned that in coming late to the meeting, you've missed an important agenda item." (say in private after the meeting)

"Perhaps you didn't realize it but the smoke is irritating some of us nearby. Would you be willing to blow the smoke in the other direction or move away from the building entrance?"

Saving Face and Softening the Sting

Reducing embarrassment is always a concern when feedback must be given, especially in a rather delicate situation. These might include feedback regarding an assortment of scenarios such as:

- Lipstick on teeth

- Unzipped fly

- Skirt in pantyhose

- Button popped on blouse

- Dragging toilet paper on bottom of shoe

- Bad Breath

- Body Odor

- Overpowering perfume/cologne

For the first several situations on this list you can refer to the top ten list. Phrase # 10 – "You may not realize…." works especially well. However, sometimes it's necessary to bring out the heavy duty "cousins" of Phrase #10 in order to "buffer" the negative comments and soften the sting:

"I thought you'd want to know…"
"I hate to have to tell you but…"
"This is difficult for me to share…"

"I have some feedback for you that you may not like..."
"I need to tell you something that you may not want to hear..."

And...for real tragedies such as downsizing, dismissals and death...

"I regret having to tell you..."
"I'm afraid I have some bad news..."
"It is with great sadness that I tell you..."

Don't Ask, Don't Tell

There are a variety of occasions when you may be ASKED for your feedback...and would rather not share it. Again the question arises: what do you say when what you have to say is not so nice?

Just for fun —and hopefully of some value too — here are possible ways to respond to these tough questions without ruining the relationship. And, without getting yourself in big trouble! I hope you'll permit me a little bit of humor and a small dose of sarcasm (allowable in these situations).

QUESTION: "Honey, what are you thinking about?"

You reply:"I was thinking about how fortunate I was to have met you." Or...

"I was daydreaming about the day we met."

QUESTION: "Do I look fat?"

You reply:"You always look perfect to me!" Or…

"Fat is such an ugly word!"

QUESTION: "What do you think of my idea?" (and you hate it!)

You reply: "I would have never thought of that." Or…

"It might not have been my first choice."

QUESTION: "Wasn't that a wonderful presentation (program, performance, play, etc)?"

You reply: "I'll have to give that some thought." Or…

"It was unlike anything I've seen before."

QUESTION: "How do you like my new… (house, car, boyfriend, hair cut etc…)"

You reply: "The question is how do YOU like it?"
(My 14 year old used this one on ME!) Or…

"I can tell that you are very happy with your choice."

WARNING: Anything you say in response to this next question may come back to haunt you.

QUESTION: "What do you think of ..." (fill in name of co-worker, boss, etc...)

You reply: "I'm getting the impression that YOU have some opinions of him." Or...

"I don't have time to think about her; I'm too busy thinking about what I have to do today!"

QUESTION: "What do you think about what happened today to... (fill in name)?"

You reply: "I'm not even going to go there!" Or...

"That's dangerous territory; think I'll stay away from that."

RECAP – Chapter 4: The Bearer of Bad News

I. Top 10 Positive Communication Phrases

- **Give benefit of the doubt...**

10. "You may not realize..."
9. "Are you aware of the effect...?"

- **Seek input...**

8. "Help me understand"
7. "I need your help"
6. "I noticed...and I'm wondering"
5. "Would you be willing to...?"

- **Take responsibility...**

4. "I'm concerned..."
3. "I would appreciate..."

- **Work together...**

2. "How can we resolve this...?"
1. "What will it take...?"

2. Feedback Do's and Don'ts – How do you rate?

Do have a sense of humor
Don't use sarcasm

3. Saving Face & Softening the Sting

To "buffer" negative comments, use phrase #10 above and related phrases such as: "Thought you'd want to know…," "I regret having to tell you…"

4. Don't Ask, Don't Tell

When ASKED for your feedback and you'd rather not share it, remember that everything you say can come back to haunt you. Use the comebacks and comments in this section carefully!

CHAPTER 5

An Offer You Can Refuse

How to set boundaries when others make demands

"Take care to get what you like or you will be forced to like what you get."   - George Bernard Shaw

How to pull rank when you have no rank to pull

Drawing boundaries and saying "no" is most challenging when the person making the request is your boss. Or, an equally powerful person: the client. It can be quite intimidating to consider refusing a request from either of these high ranking people because they seem to hold your fate in the palm of their hands.

However, you stand to suffer greater consequences if you don't set boundaries with these people. Attempting to add their requests to your already overloaded "to-do" list could result in outcomes that either reflect poorly on you or, worse, negatively affect you. Failing to set boundaries could result in:

- Poor quality work

- Last minute reneging on your promise when you just can't get it done

- Other projects suffering

- Your own suffering...mental and physical exhaustion

- Other people suffering when you're cranky and in stress overload mode

So, what do you do? When you have "no rank to pull," your best bet is to seek input, gain clarification and propose alternatives. A good example of that is phrase #5 - "Would you be willing to..." from the Top Ten Phrases list in Chapter 4. Other related phrases include:

"Would you consider...?"
"What do you think about...?"
"Would it be possible to...?"
"Could you live with it if...?"
"What if...?"
"How about...?"
"How would you feel about...?"
"Would you be open to...?"
"Would it work for you if we...?"
"Would you be OK with...?"

A print shop where I used to have my brochures and other printed materials done had a sign over the door that warned customers: "Lack of planning on your part does not constitute an emergency on my part!"

Unfortunately, you may find yourself in a situation where someone has failed to plan and then makes demands on you when he or she goes into "emergency mode." Although you may want to please customers and bosses and meet their needs, you don't want suffering –your own or quality of your work – in attempting to meet the demands.

That's when some of the phrases above come in handy. For example, say to the client:

"Would you be willing to wait until Monday morning if we hand deliver your order?" or "Could you live with it if we finished it up first thing tomorrow instead of 5pm today?" or "We're finishing up other jobs right now. How about we get started on your requests right after lunch?"

Similarly, you can use the phrases above when a boss or "higher up" in the organization asks something of you. For example:

"I'm working on your other three urgent projects today.
Would you be OK with me getting this new project to you by lunch time tomorrow?"

"Would it work for you to receive the info you need by tomorrow morning?"

"Would it be possible to get this report to you first thing next week instead of Friday afternoon?"

As I'm sure you've already guessed, the boss or client can choose not to go along with your proposed alternative. That's when you may find yourself needing to get clarification and/or seek input. You'll notice that even more phrases from the Top

Ten List in Chapter 4 – "I would appreciate..." and "I'm concerned..." – would work. Examples include:

"I would really appreciate the extra time to do the best job possible. Would you be willing to reconsider?"

"I'm concerned that the 5pm deadline won't allow us to gather all the necessary information."

"I'm concerned that working on this project today will delay the other projects that we're already working on for you. Which one is your highest priority?"

Say No Nicely – At Work

If you can't say something nice, what do you say?...especially when you get an offer –or request – that you want to refuse at work. The dilemma: How do you meet your own needs without jeopardizing your job or your business? Let's look at a couple of typical business related scenarios and possible ways to say "no" nicely.

- **"Let's do lunch!"** (and you don't want to)

One of the true tests of tact is being able to say no to a lunch invitation by a colleague, prospective client or other person with whom you really do not want to have lunch. Let's face it. Most of us guard our 168 hours per week jealously. And – rightly so – we should dole out lunch/meeting time carefully. You may find it useful to ask yourself the "W.I.I.F.M." question. That's, "WHAT'S IN IT FOR ME?" Here are three factors that may also be helpful in deciding whether or not to "do lunch":

1. Will having lunch or a face-to-face meeting with that person be beneficial in some way? ...even if that benefit is just personal enjoyment.

2. Could the conversation with that person be just as easily accomplished through some other method? I recall a potential client who suggested that I drive three hours one way to meet with him. Fortunately, he was open to my suggestion that we have a conference call instead. Phrases provided above were useful. (i.e. - "Would you consider a conference call instead of face-to-face meeting?") And, I still got the client's business!

3. Finally, does this meeting represent something that is a current priority for you? For example, I recently "did lunch" with a financial planner to discuss retirement plans for the self employed. At the time, that topic was of interest to me. Normally, I meet quite a few financial planners at the many networking meetings I attend. They all seem to be well trained to follow up with an invitation to buy lunch and discuss their services, and I typically decline. It would be easy to make excuses:

"I'm too busy."
"I'll think about it."
"I have to get back to you."
"Call me later."

But you'll eventually end up backed into a corner, undressed of all excuses. And worse, you'll end up at yet another lunch meeting that's not serving you.

Instead, try one of the following responses below to decline requests to go to lunch (and breakfast, and dinner...):

"I'm flattered that you'd like to have lunch with me. However, I'm going to choose to pass."

"I'm a little overdosed on lunch meetings. Let's schedule a time to chat on the phone."

"Being treated to lunch is quite tempting. But I think I'm going to resist the temptation."

"The subject of financial planning (fill in the blank with topic) hasn't come up on my radar screen so I think I'll opt out of the lunch opportunity."

"I appreciate the offer. However I would prefer that you email me the information instead (only if you really want the info)." Otherwise say:

"I appreciate the offer, but I'll pass."

Here's another work-related scenario and solutions. Choose the replies you can use.

- **"I need you to join my committee."**

Possible responses:

"I'm flattered that you'd like me to be part of your committee. However, I'm going to choose to pass."

"It's nice to be needed. Unfortunately, I need to focus on other areas."

"I can't join your committee. What I can do is offer you... (resources or funding, or staff support, or...)."

"I appreciate your considering me. However, I need to decline."

Say "No" Nicely – Outside the Workplace

Refusing an offer outside of the workplace can be just as challenging as saying "no" at work. Here are a few personal scenarios and solutions:

• **"Would you like to go out with me?"**

That's a tough offer to refuse without hurting the other person's feelings. And being direct is certainly braver than making excuses. Excuses such as....

"I have to wash my hair."
"I already have plans."
"I'm not available."

and the worst of all...

"I have to visit my sick grandmother."

These excuses will get you off the hook...temporarily. At some point you will run out of excuses and have to face the situation head on. So why not bite the proverbial bullet the first time you're asked? It's a lot less awkward if you respectfully decline now rather than attempting to say no later after a litany of excuses.

Here's the key. Acknowledge the other person AND also say no. Following are some possible responses. Choose the ones that you can use with a straight face. Sincerely, that is. Remember the goal: Acknowledge the other person and choose to refuse.

"I bet you could show me a great time, yet I'm going to choose to pass."

"I enjoy our current relationship and prefer to keep things the way they are."

"I know it will be my loss and I'm going to pass."

"You're a great guy (or gal), and I'm afraid that I wouldn't appreciate you as much as you deserve to be appreciated."

"You're a great person! However, I'm just not feeling any chemistry between us."

Let's look at another challenging personal scenario and solutions:

- **"Can I borrow some money?"**

"Exactly how much money are we talking about?" may be your first thought. And there's nothing wrong with lending the money...IF you're comfortable doing so. In fact, ALL of the offers discussed in this chapter could be very reasonable requests

IF you feel that you want to take them up on the offers. That's very different from saying yes when you really want to say no.

The goal is to show that you care AND at the same time choose to refuse. I call this the "empathy plus no" strategy.

Here are some possibilities:

"I know the money situation is tough. Unfortunately, I don't feel comfortable loaning the money."

"I will do whatever I can to help you but it will need to be in a non-monetary way."

"I make it a policy never to loan money." Please let me know what I can do to help in other ways."

"I know that the money would really help you. And, I feel bad because I've chosen to make it a habit never to loan money."

"I'm flattered that you would come to me for help and I regret that I won't be able to."

- **"I've recommended you for a great opportunity."**

Possible responses (including the optional phrases):

"I appreciate your thinking of me. However, I need to decline. OPTIONAL: "Could you double check with me next time before submitting my name?"

"Thanks for putting in the good word. However, I'm going to pass on this opportunity." OPTIONAL: "Let me know in advance next time and I might be able to recommend others if I can't do it."

"I'm not available, although I'm certainly flattered that you thought of me." OPTIONAL: "In the future, it might work out better if you check my availability ahead of time."

"I don't really have a strong interest in that, so I think I'll opt out of the opportunity." OPTIONAL: "Could you do me a favor next time and see if I'm interested before recommending me?"

It's important to note here that maintaining a positive tone of voice with no sarcasm is important in successfully using the "optional" phrases above. Actually, that's probably a good rule of thumb when using most phrases. See Chapter 4 for more on sarcasm. Body language and tone of voice are addressed in Chapter 7.

The "Why" Question

"Why?!!" That's the question that will most likely trip you up in choosing to refuse. You say: "I've chosen to pass on that opportunity." They say: "Why?" You say: "No thank you. I'm comfortable with the way things are." They say: "Why?" And on and on it goes. It's very easy at this point to digress into "justification" or "excuse making" mode. And, by default, it's also tempting to reach for one of those convenient, ready made excuses. Then, we're right back to the "sick grandmother" excuse all over again. Instead, when someone questions your decision, simply use one of the follow up phrases below:

"It seems to make sense to me."

"It seems like the best decision for me."

"That's just what I've chosen to do."

"It feels right."

"The little voice in the back of my head tells me it's the right decision."

"I just have a feeling about these things."

And my all time favorite:

"Why not?"

RECAP – Chapter 5: An Offer You Can Refuse

I.   How to pull rank when you have no rank to pull

Remember…when you don't draw boundaries with others there may be suffering: yours, others' and quality of work.

Seek input, gain clarification and propose alternatives in order to set limits with others.

2. Say "No" Nicely – At Work

Propose alternatives

Ask yourself what's in it for you to say yes

3. Say "No" Nicely – Outside of the Workplace

Acknowledge the other person AND refuse the request

Show you care AND refuse the request

4. The "Why" Question

When others question your choices by asking "why" use phrases that reaffirm your decision: "It seems to make sense to me", "It feels right" and "Why not?"

Avoid excuse making

CHAPTER 6

Family Dearest

How to handle nasty comments from well meaning family and friends

"Courage is the price that life exacts for granting peace."
—Amelia Earhart

It's not about you

Family. You can't live with them. And you can't get rid of them! Although you might secretly wish that you could trade them in for a new model family, you're really just left with the option of figuring out how to deal with the family you've been given.

This chapter will prepare you with phrases and comebacks for all the well-intentioned and sometimes hurtful or discouraging comments that family members have been known to make. And, while we're at it, we'll include close friends and others who seem to have your best interests at heart. The key: How to respond without ruining the relationship.

The most empowering assumption that you can make when you're on the receiving end of a nasty comment is that it's NOT ABOUT YOU! The other person's comments may be prompted by any number of emotions or intentions including:

- Caring
- Envy
- Jealousy
- Resentment
- Ego
- Control
- Concern/Worry
- Disappointment

While you may feel bad being on the receiving end of these emotions, you might also need to remind yourself that you are not responsible for others' emotions. Family and friends often attempt to make us the recipients of their angst, especially if their discontent is due to our choosing a different course of action than they would have chosen for us. Hmmm… now there's a thought worth pondering!

For example, I remember being on the receiving end of some well-meaning remarks from my parents. Several years ago one of my major training contracts was cancelled. The first words out of my parents' mouths, "I guess now you're going to get a real job!" I had to remind myself that they had still not quite gotten over the fact that I had left the very secure world of university administration to venture out into the self-employed —and less secure — world of speaking and training. And most important, I had to remind myself not to take their comments personally. Their comments were obviously a result of their concern for my well-being.

Brave, Braver or Bravest

I think that it takes guts to be able to take the high road when responding to ugly remarks made by others...and not digress into an argument or power struggle with that person. And, it takes guts to keep from slinking away passively without any response. We'll look at how to respond to such comments as "Why don't you get a real job!", "You never were the smart one were you!", "I told you so" and "Who do you think you are?"

The type of response that you choose depends upon how brave you are. In that respect, I would propose three categories of responses: brave, braver and bravest! Let's look at each of these.

Option one is BRAVE:

I refer to this first response option as "the look." This is the look that my father used to give us when we would become unruly at the dinner table. You know the one — a sideways glance with eyebrow lifted and an icy stare. The look hinted at -- even warned of -- punishments that would surely await us if we didn't "straighten up." The "look" can also be used to imply "that comment is not even worth my replying." Or, to use a popular expression "don't even go there!" This is the easiest of all choices because it doesn't require any actual verbal response. It's also great because it can be used instead of replying at any time during a conversation...especially if anything you might say would throw the interaction into a downward spiral.

Option two is <u>BRAVER:</u>

Make a clever remark in response to the person's comment. This is useful when you're in public or don't have the time or inclination to get into what the person really meant by the comment. However, there are a couple shortcomings to this strategy:

1) Most people seem to come up with wonderfully clever responses...later! In the moment that you receive a nasty comment from someone you may discover that your mind draws a total blank.

2) The second shortcoming of this strategy is that the clever responses may sound sarcastic or even antagonistic. If so, you will find that you have fallen into the "pit of ugliness" right along with the instigator.

We'll look at a number of quick one-liner comebacks that those of you who are feeling braver can use. As you've already heard in previous chapters, the secret is being ever vigilant about the tone of voice that you're using.

Option three is <u>BRAVEST:</u>

Respond by commenting on what you think the person actually meant by the comment. Or ask questions to clarify the other person's intent. This is indeed the bravest choice of all. It could open the proverbial Pandora's box of bugaboos. The question to ask yourself here is: "Do I really want to go there?" And if so, is this the right time and place to bring up all the deeply ingrained issues that might be triggering this person's comment?

Let's look at some scenarios along with possible solutions —brave, braver and bravest — that you can use. In all the scenarios below, please note that the brave option one -- giving them "the look" and saying nothing — is always a possible choice. The responses provided fit into the braver category of one-liner comebacks and the bravest category — finding out what's prompting the comment.

VERBAL ATTACKS

- "You never were the smart one were you?"

Possible responses:

Braver
"That's certainly a matter of opinion."
"We can't all be good at everything."
"And I thought I could count upon your vote of confidence."
"Sounds like I should cancel your membership in my fan club."

Bravest
"That sounded like an insult. Is that how you intended it?"
"I'm disappointed that you think so little of me."
"Can you be more specific?"

- **"Wow, you've put on some weight!"**

Possible responses:

Braver
"Actually, I haven't gained weight at all."
"If I had, I certainly wouldn't want it announced far and wide."
"Compared to whom?"
Bravest
"I didn't realize you were keeping such a close eye on my weight."
"You sound concerned. What about my weight bothers you?"

•   **"You should be more like... (your sister, brother, cousin, etc...)"**

Possible responses:

Braver
"Why mess with perfection?"
"I enjoy being just like myself."
"'Should' is such an ugly word."
"I prefer that you not 'should' on me."
"I don't think I'll sign on for that plan."
"I vote for staying just the way I am."

Bravest
"Does that mean that you find me lacking in some way?"
"What specifically is your concern about the way I am?"

•   **"Are you crazy!"**

Possible responses:

Braver

"I haven't been diagnosed yet, but I'm guessing NO."

"Depends on what you mean by 'crazy'."

"What are the symptoms?"

"If I were, would I know it?"

"Something tells me that you have an opinion on that."

Bravest

"Shall I conclude that you don't agree with my idea?"

"Can you be more specific?"

"Can you elaborate?"

- **"Who do you think you are?"**

Possible responses:

Braver

"If I guess correctly will you let me know?"

"Not think, I know who I am."

"I'm (your name). And that's my final answer."

Bravest

"Sounds like you have some concerns about something I've done."

"Why do you ask?"

CRITICISM OF YOUR CHOICES

- "Why don't you get a REAL job!"

Possible responses:

Braver
"Depends on what you mean by a real job!"

Bravest
"I'm happy with my choice of job. Isn't that what really matters?"
"Sounds like you disapprove of my career choice."
"I thought you'd be pleased that I've found work that makes me happy."
"You've always encouraged me to follow my dreams."
"I'm disappointed that you aren't supporting my career decision."

- **"What were you thinking, when you…"**
(got that haircut, picked that outfit, made that decision, chose that car, etc..)

Possible responses:

Braver
"Is that a compliment or an insult?"
"I was thinking that I made the best decision for me."
"Sounds like our tastes differ."

Bravest

"Shall I assume that you disapprove?"
"I'm getting the impression that you have some feedback for me, correct?"

- **"If those were my children, I would….**
(not let them stay up so late, not let them watch so much TV, not let them eat sweets, ….)"

Possible responses:

Braver
"Good thing there's no one right way to raise children."
"I can understand your interest in my children's well-being."
"My children would be glad to know that you're looking out for them."
"'If' is the operative word here."

Bravest
"Sounds like our child rearing opinions differ."
"I guess we'll have to agree to disagree on the way I'm raising my children."

- **"You should get rid of that girlfriend/boyfriend."**

Possible responses:

Braver
"Does that mean that we shouldn't invite you to the wedding?"
"Is that your final answer?"
"I'll tell him/her not to take it personally."
"Fortunately, I get to cast that vote."

"You're voting him/her off the island already?"
"Based on what grounds?"

Bravest
"Can you be more specific?"
"I like him/her. Isn't that all that matters?"
"You obviously have concerns. What are they?"

• **"When are you going to get married?"**

Possible responses:

Braver
"When the time is right."
"When I find Mr./Ms. Right."
"Sounds like I'm delaying YOUR timeline."
"Fortunately, I get to decide the answer to that question."
"Are you offering matchmaking services?"

Bravest
"I didn't realize there was a deadline."
"What's your concern?"
"I prefer to operate on my own timeline."

QUESTIONING YOUR COMPETENCE

• **"I told you so!"**

Possible responses:

Braver

"You did, didn't you!'

"And you seem to be getting a great deal of satisfaction from pointing that out."

"Glad I could make your day."

"Is that 1 point for you, 0 for me?"

"It's the little things in life, isn't it?"

"Without me to harass, what would you do with yourself?"

Bravest

"Is being right that important to you?"

• **"I knew you couldn't do it"**

Possible response:

Braver

"Personally, I plan to think positively."

"I guess being right is some sort of victory for you."

"I guess my loss is your win."

"It ain't over till it's over."

"The verdict is not in yet on that."

Bravest

"Any chance I can get your support?"

"I'm disappointed that you had so little faith in me."

"It almost sounds like your being right is more important than my success."

"It's too bad that I didn't have your vote of confidence."

• **"You'll never amount to anything!"**

Possible responses:

Braver
"Don't bet the house on that!"
"Is that a prediction or a curse?"
"Until I look into your crystal ball, I'm not believing it."
"I beg to differ."

Bravest
"I'm disappointed that you think so little of me."
"Perhaps with your support, we can change the ending to that story."

- **"That's a dumb idea"**

Possible responses:

Braver
"I thought it was pretty good."
"Sorry you feel that way."

Bravest
"Dumb? Can you be more specific?"
"How do you mean?"
"What is it about the idea that you find dumb?"

How brave are YOU?

As you can guess, the list of situations is endless. But the formula remains the same. You can be:

Brave

You can choose not to "go there" by just replying with the nonverbal "look" that tells the other person that you're not getting sucked into his or her "drama." And this is also a handy option when your jaw is hanging open and you can't think of a coherent reply at the moment.

Braver

You can reply with a witty and clever comeback that shows that you can hold your own, but still says "I'm not going to get into a debate with you."

Bravest

Lastly, you can choose to get to the heart of the issue by addressing the underlying intent of what the other person has said. And since this is the bravest option of all, it may also involve your sharing your true feelings regarding the person's remark. As you observed in the responses to the scenarios, those feelings are often ones of disappointment. Sharing those feelings may be important in not taking the situation personally. And more importantly, it may be the first step toward a meaningful conversation with "family dearest" or any other well-intentioned friend or family member.

RECAP – Chapter 6: Family Dearest

I. When family and friends make nasty comments, remember: It's not about you!
    It's more about what they're experiencing – from envy and jealously to caring and concern.

2. Possible responses to negative remarks from others fall into three categories – brave, braver and bravest!

> <u>Brave</u> -   Non verbal response suggesting "don't even go there."

> <u>Braver</u> - Witty, clever reply. Be careful to go easy on the sarcasm.

> <u>Bravest</u> - Question or comment intended to understand the intent of the person's unkind remark.

3. Verbal Attacks

    Responses to such remarks as "Wow, you've put on some weight!", "Are you crazy?" and "Who do you think you are?"

4. Criticism of your choices

    Responses to remarks such as "Why don't you get a real job?", "I told you so" and "When are you going to get married?"

5. Questioning your competence

    Responses to remarks such as "I knew you couldn't do it" and "You'll never amount to anything!"

6. How brave are YOU?

    You decide how brave you are. Will you just give the dear family member or friend the "don't even go there" look? Will you use a witty come back? Or, will you explore the intent behind the nasty remark?

CHAPTER 7

You're the Boss!

How to Supervise in a Way That Gains the Cooperation of Others

"Leadership is the ability to influence others to do willingly and well that which needs to be done." — Charles Pellerin

Whatever!

Handling communication challenges takes on a whole new meaning when you're the boss. One of the biggest tests is responding to employees with negative attitudes. The demons of the "If you can't say something nice, don't say anything at all" conditioning can continue to haunt you even as a supervisor. You might be observing the negative behavior and thinking "I'd really rather not go there!" Here are a few reasons you might want to address the negative employee anyway:

- Makes the employee aware of the problem

- There may actually be improvement

- Keeps the problem from getting worse

- Reduces resentment from other employees

- Keeps negativity from becoming the norm

The tough question is "how do you quantify attitude?" The answer: link it to observable behaviors. And, most importantly, identify the negative impact of those behaviors...the impact on others in the office, the impact on the team's ability to reach its goal or the impact on the clients. The A.I.R. (Awareness – Impact – Request) Model discussed in both Chapter 1 and Chapter 3 may be helpful here.

Here are a few examples of phrases you might use to "quantify" and correct attitude issues:

"When you roll your eyes in the meeting others feel that you aren't interested in their ideas. Is that the way you really feel?"

"When you sigh heavily in front of the customers they might mistake that for impatience. I need you to refrain from doing that in the future."

"When you say 'whatever' it sets a negative tone in the office. And, others don't know what your specific concerns are when you say that. In the future I would appreciate your expressing directly what is bothering you."

Keep in mind that some employees may be hesitant to say what's bothering them because they have a history of being told that it's really not ok to say. Sometimes they need to be convinced that you really DO want to hear them out. In the next section of this chapter you'll gain strategies for conveying to employees that you want to hear what they have to say...even as you brace yourself for what they might say.

Ask for More

When I was a new supervisor, one of my mentors gave me a precious piece of advice that has served me well for over 25 years. She advised that when you receive constructive criticism or negative feedback you should ASK FOR MORE! More information, that is.

Some of my favorite phrases for "asking for more" include:

"Can you be more specific?"
"Can you give me an example?"
"Could you elaborate please?"
"Tell me more."
"How do you mean?"

And to take it one step further, you can solicit input from the person sharing the criticism by asking for his or her suggestions. These phrases include:

"What do you suggest?"
"What would you like to see happen?"
"What do you think we should do?"
"How should we resolve it?"
"In your opinion, what should be done?"

The first time I used this advice vividly stands out in my mind. When I worked in university administration, I held weekly one-on-one meetings with each member of my staff.

On one such occasion I had just come back from an off site supervisor training. The trainer had reminded us of the importance of soliciting input from our staff. Staff opinions on ways to improve the department were deemed especially important. Eager to try this out, I launched into this conversation at my one-on-one meeting:

Sarita: "Bill, how do you think we could improve our department?"

Bill: "Well, Sarita, I think YOU could be a better supervisor!"

(Long pause as Sarita fights off the urge to get defensive and "write Bill up" for insubordination. Sarita chooses the "ask for more" strategy instead.)

Sarita: "A better supervisor? How do you mean?"

Bill: "It would be helpful if you could give us more specific feedback on how we are doing."

Sarita: "What suggestions do you have?"

Bill: "Maybe, at each one-on-one meeting tell us one thing we're doing well and one thing we need to improve. Some of us are not sure how you feel about how well we're doing in our jobs."

Sarita: "I could do that. We'll start with next week's one-on-one meeting!"

The "ask for more" strategy served me well that day. (And, it continues to help me receive criticism gracefully...even as I fight the urge to cup my hands over my ears and chant "I don't hear you, I don't hear you..."). I cringe to think how that scenario with my employee might have turned out if I had instead chosen to get defensive. It certainly would have done nothing to further the positive supervisor – employee relationship.

In addition to "asking for more" information when you receive constructive criticism, it's also good practice to ask the questions below. After all, it took guts for the employee to dare to share this feedback with you. The least you could do is carefully examine it. When receiving negative feedback or constructive criticism from your employees, assume that it could be valid and ask yourself:

- Have I received this feedback before? Perhaps from other employees?

- Have I observed myself demonstrating the offending behavior?

- Is it something I want to change?

- Is it something I CAN change?

- What will I actually DO in response to this feedback?

In the example with my employee, Bill, (not his real name) suggesting that I regularly let the staff know how they were performing, I felt it was something that I wanted to and could change. Further, I had received similar feedback in the past. When I first started supervising I had foolishly announced to my staff "No news is good news!" Their reply: "If you don't tell us, we'll make something up!" And, I knew their imaginations would be way more dramatic than the reality!

So, it was not the first time I had been told by an employee I needed to do a better job of letting all of them know how they were doing. And of course, it was easier for me to put the feedback into action thanks to Bill's suggestion that I use the one-on-one meeting to give each employee well deserved kudos and suggested improvements.

One of the biggest frustrations I hear from employees who attend my seminars is that they don't feel that their supervisors really want their input, especially if they have concerns or something else "not so nice" to share. Further, they lament the fact that, even if the supervisor does listen and even write down the feedback, that they don't really act upon it. Perhaps, one of the best credibility builders for you, as a supervisor, is to give an honest reply to the employee as to what will happen to the suggestion. Then act on it! Possible replies include:

"Thank you for the suggestion. I will bring it up at the next Directors meeting."

"I appreciate the input. Although the budget is already set for this year, I will put it in the action file for next year."

"I appreciate your bringing this to my attention. I will fix the situation myself and give you an update at our next one-on-one meeting."

"I'm glad you suggested this idea. Let's bring this up at the next departmental staff meeting and brainstorm possible solutions."

Companies that are fortunate enough to be included in the book, **100 Best Companies To Work For in America** must meet several important criteria. One of these is that there is "trust" in the organization. The book's coauthor, Robert Levering, defines trust as "employees feel that their ideas are important and that their contributions matter." Fostering trust among your team is an important outcome of listening to employees and acting upon their ideas. Acknowledge the idea even if it's presented by the employee in a "borderline insubordinate" way such as "You need to be a better supervisor!"

The "ask for more" strategy can also be useful when you receive feedback from your boss. A manager in one of my seminars shared with me that she had recently received her performance review by her boss. And she was not happy about it. "You're not a team player!" was the boss' assessment of her abilities. Instead of becoming indignant and insubordinate, she shared with me that she had asked "What do I do that makes you say that?" Perfect response. She "asked for more" information instead of getting defensive.

By the way, he had said she was not a team player because she sat in staff meetings with her arms folded. "Closed body posture," he'd said. Fortunately they discussed it. And, she shared that her arms were folded not because she was "closed" but because the meeting room was cold!

Body Behavior

As we just saw in the example above, other people will draw conclusions based on your body language and other nonverbal actions. You may be familiar with the frequently quoted work of Dr. Albert Mehrabian of UCLA. His research showed that:

- Only 7% of communication is interpreted based on the actual words.

- 38% is in the tone of voice and other vocal aspects of communication.

- A whopping 55% is in the body language.

Some years ago, when the sitcom **The Nanny** was in its hey day, one of my seminar participants shared with the group that he thought the show's star Fran Drescher had made nasal (38% voice tone) fashionable. Another participant quickly chimed in with a very telling remark: "No, that's not true. What happened was that the 55% that is her body rose up and overtook the 38%." Point well taken. In fact, Fran Drescher confirmed that comment later the same week on the **David Letterman** show. When Letterman complimented her on her appearance she said in her most nasal tone "Thanks! When you sound like I do, you've gotta look good!"

The point? How you say something is important (38%). Gestures and other body language is even more important (55%). This is especially important when you are the boss. Employees will take their cue from how you say something, just as much as what you say.

Here are some additional examples of nonverbal actions and what they most commonly signal to others:

- **Nodding head = "I understand" (NOT "I agree")**

Big communication glitches can occur with the head nod. We might make the mistake of assuming that a client's nodding head means "I'm agreeing with you" or "I'm on board with your idea."

However, the person may simply be saying that he or she understands – not necessarily agrees. It may be helpful for us to actually point out what we're seeing and ask for additional feedback. For example – "I noticed you're nodding. What are your thoughts about what I've shared with you?"

- **Stroking Chin = "Contemplating"**

If we see a client or co-worker stroking his or her chin, more than likely there is some contemplation or evaluation taking place. However, we cannot presume to know the details of the deliberation. Again it may be useful for us to probe by asking the multi-purpose question already mentioned – "What are your thoughts?" or "What questions can I answer?"

- **Rolled eyes = "Disapproval"**

Non-verbal sarcasm would be the perfect way to describe this body behavior. Employees, especially, may express their disapproval and negative feelings non-verbally when they feel uncertain about whether it's safe to verbally share their thoughts. This is a perfect opportunity for us to probe further. We might say something such as "I'm getting the impression that you have concerns and I'd like to hear what you have to say."

- **Deep sighing = "Boredom" or "Impatience"**

Frequently people sigh and don't realize they're doing it. Nevertheless, it can send a loud and clear signal that something is amiss. Again, we have an opportunity to further inquire about the other person's reaction.

Phrases of Praise

A manager at a bank in Toronto shared with me that she had a wonderful overachiever on her team who consistently exceeded the department's sales goals. The manager sheepishly admitted that whenever the overachiever would share her latest record breaking achievement, the manager would say "Next time I bet you can do even more!"

It occurred to the manager that the employee would never be "good enough." She admitted that perhaps she needed to at least say a few words of acknowledgement to the overachiever before raising the bar yet again. Or, that, perhaps the bar did not even need to be raised. Considering the fact that the employee was consistently performing well above the standard, maybe she was already "good enough!"

Speaking of good enough, many employees don't receive sufficient acknowledgement and praise. A colleague shared with me that she had been working for her current employer for 15 years. And, she had not once been told by her supervisor "Thank you for doing a good job!" or anything that resembled an acknowledgement.

As a supervisor you may be so busy cranking through your own "to do" list that you don't seem to find the time to compliment the staff. That was certainly a big part of my struggle as a supervisor. I suppose the universal problem of swamped supervisors is what catapulted Ken Blanchard's book **The One Minute Manager** to the top of the best seller list in the early 1980s. His concept of "catching employees doing something right" shaped the management style of many managers.

In fact, the more specific you can be in giving praise to your employees, the better. For example:

"Great job handling the staff meeting this morning."
"I liked the way you resolved that client problem."
"Very thorough report!"

Although I'm sure employees will also appreciate a quick one or two word acknowledgement such as "Thank you" or "Appreciate it," I wish I would have had a handy "cheat sheet" or easy reference list of phrases of praise when I was a supervisor. So, for your convenience, here are some quick kudos to get you started:

"Nice Job"

"Wonderful job"

"Fantastic"

"Superb"

"Excellent"

"Nice try"

"Incredible"

"Magnificent"

"Congratulations"

"Good work"

"Super"

"You rock!"

"Awesome"

"Perfect"

"I'm proud of you"

"Love it"

"Brilliant"

"Great participation"

"Outstanding"

"You got it"

"Well done"

"Marvelous"

"Woo Hoo!"

I must confess that the phrases above were excerpted from a longer list created by my 14 year old daughter and one of her friends. I asked them to write down every word of praise they would want to hear from someone else. And, as we already know from the parenting magazines' wisdom in Chapter 2, people have been the way they are since the age of 4. I propose that the same positive strokes that make a four year old beam proudly or make a 14 year old feel special are the same words that make adults feel appreciated.

As we conclude this chapter and this book, I think the words of the late Mother Teresa say it best:

"Kind words can be short and easy to speak, but their echoes are truly endless."

RECAP – Chapter 7: You're the Boss!

I.   Remember to "quantify" negative attitude by linking it to observable behavior and identify the impact of the behavior.

2.   When you receive negative feedback, ASK FOR MORE. Use such phrases as:

"How do you mean?"
"Tell me more."
"What do you suggest?"

3.   When you receive negative feedback, thank the person for sharing it and genuinely consider it by asking yourself:

"Have I heard this feedback before?"
"Is this something I want to change?"
"Is this something I CAN change?"

4.   Remember, your employees take their cue from your body language (55%) then your tone of voice (38%) and lastly, your words (7%).

5.   Add "praise employees" to your supervisor "to do" list. Give specific praise such as "Good job handling that meeting" as well as quick one or two word kudos such as "Great job," "Terrific work" or "Awesome."

APPENDIX I

105 Phrases for All Occasions

CHAPTER I: **To Confront or Not Confront?**

1. I'm sure that it wasn't your intention to...
2. As you may already know...
3. I'm getting the impression that...
4. It seems like...
5. I worry that...
6. I feel that...
7. When you do _____ it makes me feel _____.
8. When you say_____ the way it affects the office is _____.
9. Could you please...?
10. In the future I would like you to...
11. Next time I would appreciate...
12. I really need your help with...
13. I would rather you...
14. Would it be possible to...
15. Let's...
16. Can we...

CHAPTER 2:   **Is the Glass Half Empty or Half Full?**

17. She's not a pest; she's persistent.
18. He's not a penny pincher; he's efficient

19. Is this really about me?
20. This too shall pass.
21. Does it matter in the big picture?
22. When they record the history of time, will this event be documented?
23. They've been this way since they were four years old!
24. What are the options?
25. What's in it for me?

CHAPTER 3: From Conflict to Collaboration

26. What's the real agenda?
27. I feel like there's more to this than meets the eye.
28. I feel like there's something else bothering you.
29. How can we make this work?
30. What do you need from me?
31. Could you live with it if we...?
32. How might we gain your cooperation?
33. What do you think about...?
34. What's plan b?

CHAPTER 4: The Bearer of Bad News

35. You may not realize...
36. Are you aware of the effect?
37. Help me understand...
38. I need your help.
39. I noticed...and I'm wondering...
40. Would you be willing to...
41. I'm concerned...
42. I would appreciate...

43. How can we resolve this?
44. What will it take...?
45. So what you're saying is...
46. I thought you'd want to know...
47. This is difficult for me to share...
48. I need to tell you something that you may not want to hear...
49. I regret having to tell you...
50. I'll have to give that some thought.
51. The question is how do YOU like it?

CHAPTER 5: An Offer You Can Refuse

52. Would you consider...?
53. What do you think about...?
54. Would it be possible to...?
55. Could you live with it if...?
56. What if...?
57. How about...
58. How would you feel about...?
59. Would you be open to...?
60. Would it work for you if...?
61. Would you be OK with...?
62. I appreciate the offer, but I'll pass.
63. I'm flattered that you'd like me to be part of the committee yet I'll pass.
64. I appreciate your considering me. However, I need to decline.
65. I bet you could show me a great time, but I'm going to choose to pass.

66. Thank you. I'm flattered.
67. Could you double check with me in advance next time?
68. It seems to make sense to me.
69. It seems like the best decision for me.
70. That's just what I've chosen to do.
71. It feels right.
72. Why not?

CHAPTER 6:   Family Dearest

73. Do I really want to go there?
74. That's certainly a matter of opinion.
75. I'm disappointed that you think so little of me.
76. Shall I conclude that you don't agree with my idea?
77. Sounds like you have some concerns about something I've done.
78. I'm happy with my choice. Isn't that what really matters?
79. I'm disappointed that you aren't supporting my career decision.
80. Is that a compliment or an insult?
81. Sounds like our taste differs.
82. I'm getting the impression that you have some feedback for me.
83. "If" is the operative word.
84. I didn't realize that being right was so important to you.
85. Any chance I can get your support?
86. I beg to differ.
87. What is it about the idea that you find dumb?

CHAPTER 7:   You're the Boss!

88. When you say "whatever" it sets a negative tone in the office.
89. When you roll your eyes in the meeting others feel that you aren't interested.
90. How do you mean?
91. Can you be more specific?
92. Tell me more.
93. What do you suggest?
94. In your opinion, what should be done?
95. I'm glad you suggested the idea.
96. I appreciate your bringing this to my attention.
97. Thank you for the suggestion.
98. Have I received this feedback before?
99. Is this something I want to change?
100. Thank you for doing a good job.
101. Great job handling the staff meeting.
102. I like the way you resolved that client problem.
103. Fantastic!
104. I'm proud of you.
105. Well done!

APPENDIX II:

Team Communication--
Sarita's Top 10 Favorite Icebreakers & Get Acquainted Activities

1. **What's in your wallet?**
    Participants share an object from their wallet/ purse which represents them and explain why.

2. **Guess Who?**
    Participants write on an index card six adjectives that describe themselves. Cards are collected, shuffled and dealt. Each person reads the adjectives and attempts to identify which person in the group the card describes.

3. **Magazine Puzzle Hunt**
    This activity is used to divide your staff into smaller groups. In advance, cut magazine pages into 6-8 pieces (# of pages should equal # of groups desired). Scramble and distribute one piece to each person. Participants mingle and form groups as they put their puzzle together.

4. **Song Tunes**
    To divide your staff into smaller groups, give each participant a piece of paper with a well known but

simple song title on it (For example – Happy Birthday, Row Your Boat, Jingle Bells). Participants mingle and hum the song tune until they find other participants humming the same song.

5. **Life Line**
    Have each person draw a line on a piece of paper with 0 on far left end. Instruct each person to write on the line at least 5 significant events and at what age each occurred. Share in pairs or small group. For example:

    0 -- Spelling Bee (age12) -- College (age18) – Married (age 25) --Sales Award (age 29).

6. **M&M Sharing**
    Circulate a bag of M&Ms asking each person to take as many as they want. The number of M&Ms each person takes is how many personal facts he/she must share with the group. Best for small groups of fewer than 20 people.

7. **Truth, Truth, Lie**
    Participants write down three facts about themselves. Two facts must be true and one fact must be false. Other person(s) guesses which one of the three facts is false. Can be done in pairs or small groups.

8. **Name Game**
    Participants introduce themselves using a descriptive word that begins with same letter as their name (ex – Smiling Sarita, Sensational Susan, Perfect Paul). The real fun is that participants must repeat all of

the preceding descriptions and names prior to stating their own. This is good for newly formed groups of 30 or fewer.

9. **Human Scavenger Hunt**

    In advance, create a page of descriptions about people in the group. Some items can be very specific based on facts you know about group members; some of info can be generic. Each person must mingle and get the signature of the appropriate person/s. First one to get all items signed wins.

    For example-

    Find someone who....

    -Has been with the company more than 5 years

    -Has traveled outside of the US

    -Participates in the same hobby you do

10. **Who Am I?**

    The name of a famous person is taped on the back of each person. Participants mingle and ask each other YES or NO questions to determine the identity of the person taped to their back... (For ex – Am I a politician? Am I a woman? Am I someone who is over age 30?) You can also create a theme such as names of characters from a certain movie or TV show.

APPENDIX III

Team Trust and Communication Checklist

How well does your team communicate and promote trust? Check all that apply. I feel that team members...

A)   Listen to and value each other's opinions

B)   Help and support each other

C)   Feel comfortable approaching each other with concerns

D)   Acknowledge each other and give credit where credit is due

E)   Follow through and do what they say they're going to do

F)   Effectively resolve conflicts

G)   Accept constructive criticism without becoming defensive

H)   Keep confidential information to themselves

I)   Care about the quality of their work

J)   Remain flexible and adapt easily to changes that occur in the organization

Items that you did NOT check suggest areas for improvement. What might you do to improve team communication and trust as a team member? As a supervisor?

APPENDIX IV

7 Step Employee Feedback Plan

1. Clarify expectations

2. Specify what you want changed (Focus on behaviors)

3. Ask for employee's understanding of the situation

4. Get a commitment

5. Identify follow up plans and consequences

6. Keep a written record of the meeting

7. Reinforce employee's progress

APPENDIX V

Recommended Reading

How to Say It At Work: Putting Yourself Across with Power Words, Phrases, Body Language and Communication, Jack Griffin, Prentice Hall, 1998.

How to Say It Best: Choice Words, Phrases, & Model Speeches for Every Occasion, Jack Griffin, Prentice Hall, 1994.

Crucial Conversations: Tools for Talking When Stakes are High, Kerry Patterson, et al, McGraw-Hill, 2002.

Fierce Conversations: Achieving Success at Work and in Life, One Conversation at a Time, Susan Scott, Viking, 2002.

Difficult Conversations: How to Discuss What Matters Most, Douglas Stone, et al of the Harvard Negotiation Project. Viking, 1999.

Magic Words, Howard Kaminsky and Alexandra Penney, Broadway Books, 2002.

Dealing With People You Can't Stand, Rick Brinkman and Rick Kirschner, McGraw Hill, 2002.

What You Say Is What You Get: How to Master Power Talking, the Language of Success, George Walther, Berkeley, 2002.

Learned Optimism: How to Change Your Mind and Your Life, Martin Seligman, Ph.D, Picket Books, 1993.

What You Can Change and What You Can't, Martin Seligman, Ph.D., Knopf, 1994.

Feel The Fear and Do It Anyway, Susan Jeffers, Ph.D., Ballantine, 1987.

Getting Past No: Negotiating Your Way From Confrontation to Cooperation, William Ury, Bantam, 1993.

Talking From 9 to 5 (How Women's and Men's Conversational Styles Affect Who Gets Heard, Who Gets Credit and What Gets Done at Work), Deborah Tannen, Ph.D., Morrow, 1994.

Communicating Effectively for Dummies, Marty Brounstein, Hungry Minds, Inc, 2001.

How to Get Along With Difficult People, Florence Littauer, Harvest House, 1999.

The One Minute Manager, Kenneth Blanchard, Ph.D., Spencer Johnson, Berkley Books, 1982.

The Four Agreements, Don Miguel Ruiz, Amber-Allen Publishing, Inc., 1997.

Mary Kay on People Management, Mary Kay Ash, Warner Books, 1985.

The 100 Best Companies to Work for in America, Robert Levering, Milton Moskowitz, 1994.

The Dilbert Principle, Scott Adams, Harper Business, 1996.

Resources featuring Sarita Maybin include:

Motivational CD **Turning Negativity into Possibilities**, produced by Inspired Life Development, 2003.

Contributing Author, **Career Compass for Women**, a women's leadership book endorsed and promoted by the American Business Women's Association , Maracom Publishing, 2003.

Contributing author of **The Productivity Path: Your Roadmap for Improving Employee Performance**, Maracom Publishing, 2001.

Four volume video program entitled **How to Discipline Employees and Correct Performance Problems,** produced by Career Track Seminars, 1996.

Made in the USA
San Bernardino, CA
04 April 2018